Kids Say the Darndest Things
Teacher Edition

By Shondra M. Quarles

All Rights Reserved. © Copyright Shondra M. Quarles 2023
Disclaimer
No part of this book may be reproduced or transmitted in any form or by any means, mechanical or electronic, including photocopying or recording, or by an information storage and retrieval system, or transmitted by e-mail without permission in writing from the publisher. This book is for entertainment purposes only.
The views expressed are those of the author alone.

"If we all could see the world through the eyes of a child, we would see the magic in everything."
~Chee Vai tang

Growing Pains

My legs were hurting last night. It's because I was growing up.

Christmas Confessions

Dear Santa,
I been good and naughty. I been both!

The Good Life

When is the parent conference? Yes! I have a little more time to act good.

Little Leaders

Whenever you need us, whenever, we'll always be there for you.

Nursery Rhyme Remix

The farmer takes a life. farmer takes a life. High-ho the derry-oh the farmer takes a life.

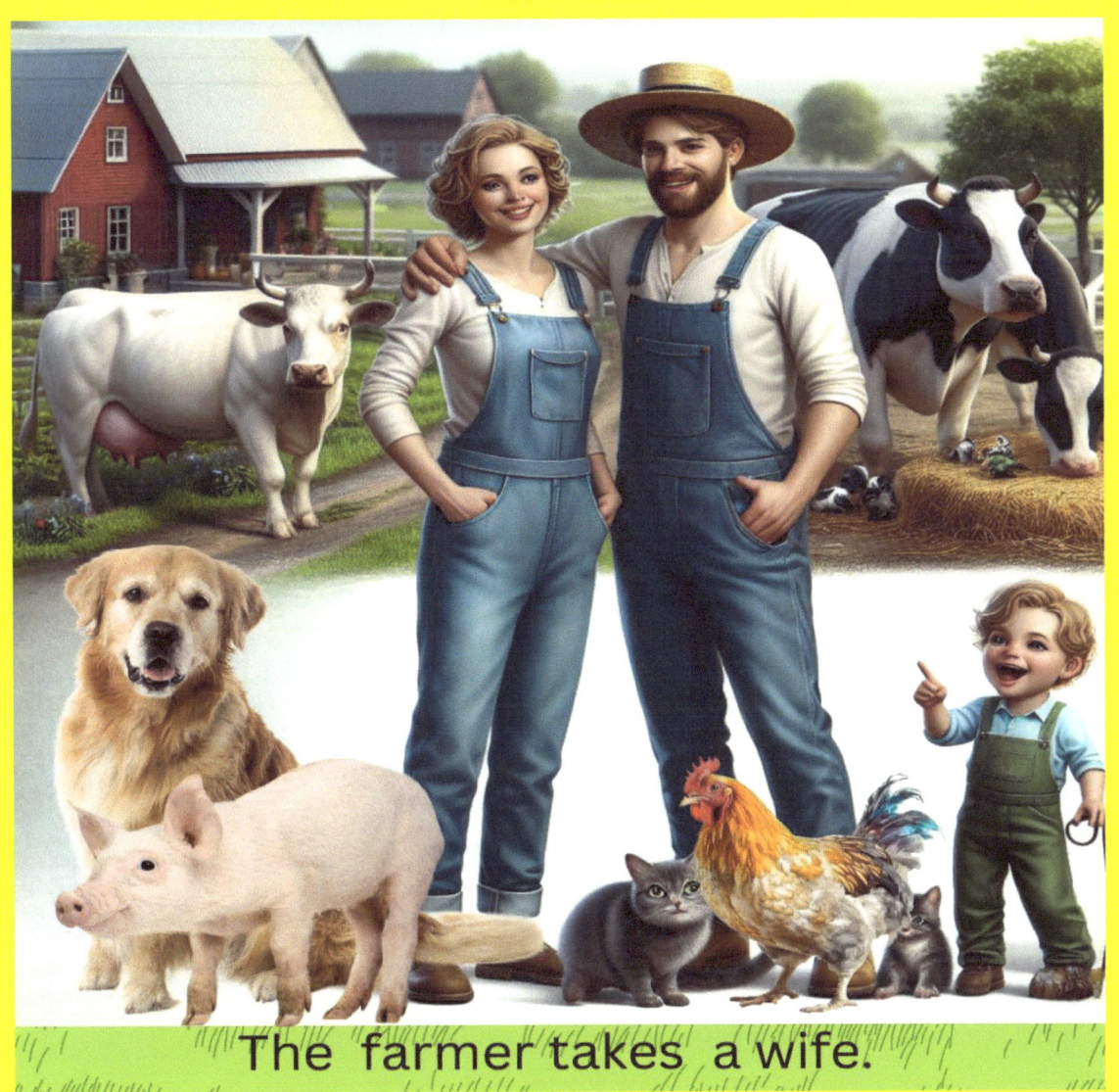

The farmer takes a wife.

Seasonal Allergies

I'm allergic to Santa Claus. When I open my presents, I'm gonna sneeze.

A Feathery Feast

See this red bump? I poisoned myself last night because I ate chicken. Some chicken has poison. It still has the feathers. I don't like the feathers, but I wanna fly!

Cheesy Beginnings

My tia ate cheese, and now she's pregnant! It's because she ate old cheese.

Beans and Mice

If mice eat beans, does that mean they don't eat *CHEESE* anymore?

Empty Purse, Full Heart

You're broke? I think you need to save some income for lunch!

Mr. Big Spender

It's okay, Mr. Brown. I'll pay for it.
I don't care about my money!

Whiz Kid

Good job! See what happens when you hang out with me! I'm a *BIG* expert.

E for Effort

Jake's on it! First, he was lazy. Now, he's smart!

Mystery Number

My mom says I'm *NOT* nineteen; I'm five.

U is for Underwear

Teacher:
When you were babies, you wore diapers. Now, you wear underwear. We all do.

Butter-fumble

He dropped the football because he had butterfingers. 'Butterfingers' means you have butter all over your fingers.

Little Independent Minds

We don't need you to help us. We got it!

Term of Endearment

I put my sentence as, 'Hi Boo' because Black ladies say, 'Hi, Boo.'

Name Whiz

I've been knowing how to spell my name for 100 years.

Ph is for Phonics

Ph sounds like a flat tire-fffffff!

My Favorite Book is Facebook

I go to my mom's Facebook to see what's going on!

Text Tales

Hey, I'm going to text you, okay? Now, you text me. Use your imagination.

Imaginary Snapshots

You want me to Facebook this?

Free-Choice

Yes! I can go to the computer. I'm free to go wherever I want to go. Abraham Lincoln signed the Emancipation Proclamation for *ME*!

The Science of Healing

Nurses are scientists; they just know when kids feel better.

Do You Hear What I Hear?

My uncle has big ears like me and big eye lashes.

Farewell Founding Father

Well, what I learned is George Washington died. Maybe because he was too old.

V is for Vet

We should be happy that Mr. Wilson is a veterinarian because whenever our puppies are hurt, we can tell him at our school.

Gentle Guidance

I have a question: Why did his dad push him to do better? My parents *NEVER* push me!

Kindergarten Laws

1. Don't shoot nobody.
2. Don't go past stop signs.
3. And *DON'T WALK IN THE STREETS WITHOUT PANTS!*

Grandma Knows Best

My Grandma is nosey. She wants to know *EVERYTHING* we do at *MY* house!

A Slice of Joy

I like Chuck E. Cheese. It reminds me of happy moments, like when I was a little baby and used to hug my dad!

Attitude is Everything

I want to play my Xbox, but my dad tells me no because he's watching the game. Sometimes I just don't like my dad's attitude!

Key to a Broken Heart

Teacher, my heart is back together again because I get to see my family!

Beast Mode

When my mom yells, she turns into a BEAST.

Kindergarten Cop

My mom is a *BOSSY COP*. She tells me un-tuck your shirt. Do this. Do that.

Financial Literacy

My mommy doesn't have any money. She just borrows my dad's.

Baby Talk

I don't like it when my parents call me baby. I just go with it, but I don't like it!

Date Night Adventure

My mom and dad took a trip. That's a date.

Daddy Duty

I wanna be a seahorse because the *BOYS* have the babies. Then *WE* don't have to worry about that.

Class Clown

You're funny, but you don't wanna be the clown.

Timeless Teacher

My teacher can't be 100 years old. If he was that old, he'd be dead already!

Brainiac

I'm a really smart boy. My brain is growing. That's why I have a big head.

Sizing Up

Teacher, my sister will buy me a book from the book fair. She is eight. She is flat just like you. 'Flaaat' means skinny.

The Great Pretender

Janiyah is crying, but she is just acting. One day she's gonna be on the stage.

Sub Factory

My teacher is sick. I think she will have to be replaced.

Cheer Leader

I know what's gonna happen if we don't follow the rules. We are gonna have another pep talk!

Critter Chronicles

There was a alien bug in my classroom today. My teacher destroyed it!

Go EJ!

It's DJ, not EJ!

Resting Sole

My feet is sleeping. It's tired because it didn't go to sleep last night.

The Art of Sharing

Let's switch colors. Me and Tommy are great switchers.

Shoo Fly

I said, 'Shoo Fly', and it's still bothering me.

Teacher's Pet

That's okay, Ms. Jackson. Everyone makes mistakes. Just don't forget to take attendance tomorrow.

The Joy of Triumph

I didn't cry today during the fire drill. It's just practice, and *PRACTICE MAKES PERFECT*.

The Joy of Learning

I like school. Whenever I learn, it makes me feel happy!

Teaching is a Work of Heart

Teaching isn't about making money, Mr. Jay. It's about helping kids.

H is for Hero

My teacher wants us to be safe with scissors. She says it could save your life. Uh oh, somebody's a hero.

Boy's Best Friend

I wish I had a dog so he could eat my homework.

The Weary Tooth Fairy

I can't believe I got one hundred dollars from my Tooth Fairy. I looked at the one and saw two zeroes. Something must be wrong with my Tooth Fairy.

School is My Job

Everyone is thanking me for helping them. That's why I'm *EMPLOYEE OF THE MONTH*.

Little Einsteins

Student:
Hey, remember, our principal wants us to be *FRANKENSTEINS*.
Teacher:
No sweetie, that's *EINSTEINS*!

Back in the Day

The 80's is the olden days. All the pictures were in black and white. That's old school.

Start at the Beginning

Teacher: Let's write a formal letter. It's been a while since I've handwritten a letter. I almost don't remember how to start.

Student: I know how to start. You start with an UPPER CASE letter.

Hugs Are for Saving

I don't have any hugs. They're my moms.

Respecting Boundaries

Stop it! You need to listen to what she is saying. Stop means stop, and Go means go.

Offspring

Teacher, my mom reproduced. She has babies.

Forget Me Not

Ms. Smith, You forgot to put 'and fish', after they eat seals. But that's okay, just put, 'OH I FORGOT AND FISH!'

Bossing Up Through Education

Well, if you don't like people telling you what to do, finish school and go to college. Then, you can grow up and tell people what to do.

Nature's Beauty

Those bumps are pimples.

Speeding Lessons

Yeah, I told my dad you got caught by the cops. What did the judgemet say?

Pass the Gas

Ewww, Mrs. Harris farted. Do girls even do that?

Hair-Raising Education

Your arm looks like it has a mustache.

He Loves Me Not

Student: Dad, remember you love my teacher? You love her, you love her…
Dad: She's crazy!
Teacher: Yes! She is crazy!

Free Elsa

Elsa got arrested. I saw it on Facebook when the cops put her in handcuffs. Maybe she will get out of jail in time for my party. My mom already invited her because my party is gonna be a Frozen party. Awww, poor Elsa!

A Shopping We Will Go

Those are so cute, Ms. Q. Did your baby daddy buy you those boots?

It's in the Title

Teacher: Someone left their underpants on the carpet!
Student: She said underpants!

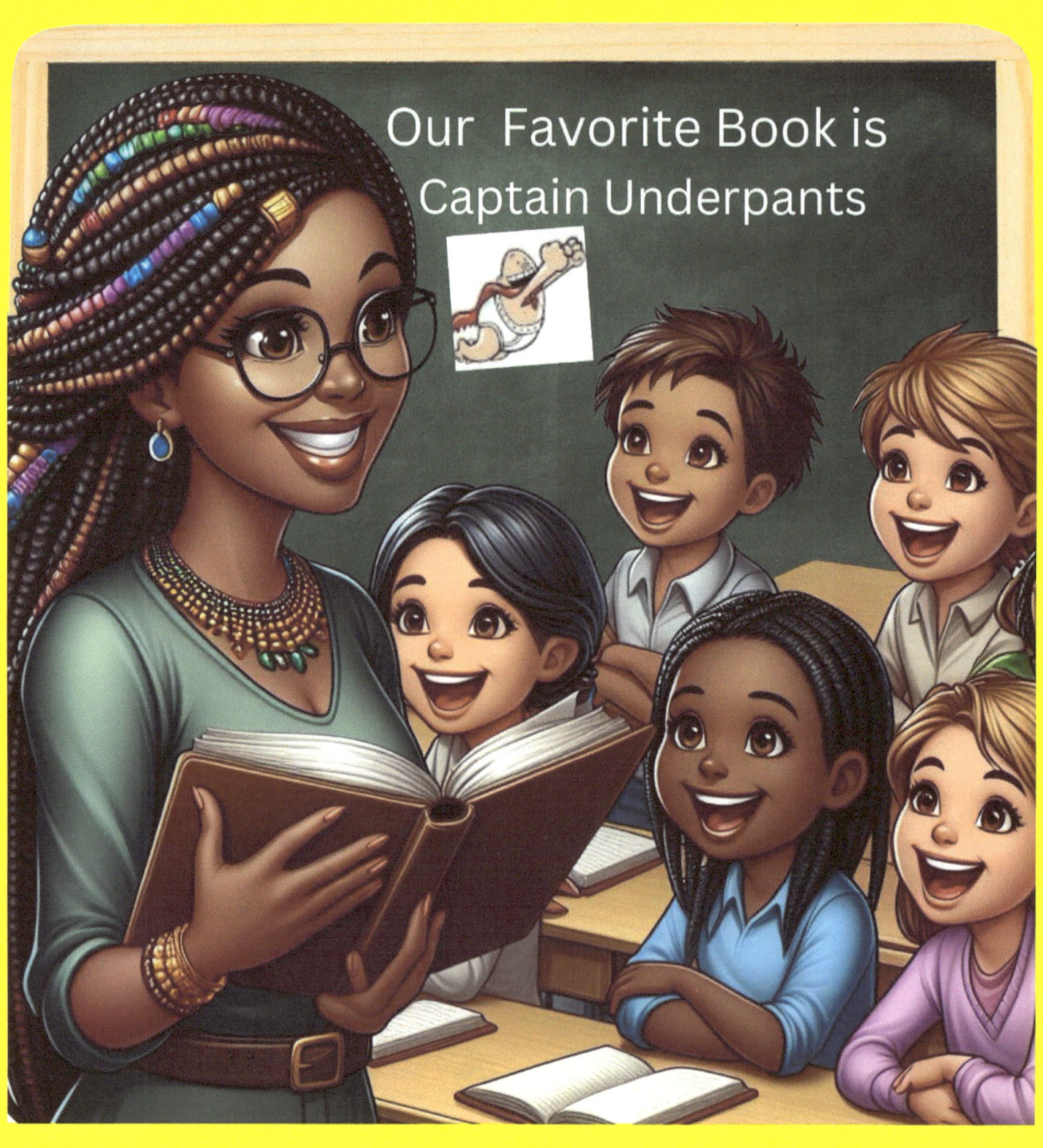

Mammal Mystery

Girls are mammals, but boys are *NOT* mammals because we don't make milk or babies. My dad didn't lay babies!

Baby's Day Out

Boy: Mi Pansa!
Girl: He says his tummy hurts. It's the baby. He wants to come out.

The Beauty of Motherhood

My mom looks prettiest when she is WEIRD.

Purr-fect Love

I know who Cat in the Hat's wife is. Cat Woman!

A Delicious Career Choice

When I grow up, I want to be a donut!

The End?

Copyright © Shondra M. Quarles
Author and Digital Design December 29, 2023

Eye Heart Literacy, LLC
Contact Information:
Eyeheartliteracy@gmail.com
https://eyeheartliteracy.carrd.co/.